_____

By

_____

On the Occasion of

_____

Date

_____

Several text selections were compiled from the following: *In Celebration of a New Day*, *365 Days of Purpose for Women*, *365 Days of Wisdom for Busy Women*, *365 Days of Hope*, *365 Prayers for Women*, *365 Encouraging Words for Women*, *365 Inspirational Quotes*, *365 Favorite Quotes for Dads*, *365 Favorite Quotes for Grandmothers*, *365 Favorite Quotes for Friends*, *365 Inspiring Moments for Teachers*, *365 Moments of Peace for Moms* published by Barbour Publishing, Inc.

Scripture quotations marked NIV are taken from the HOLY BIBLE, NEW INTERNATIONAL VERSION®. NIV®. Copyright © 1973, 1978, 1984 by International Bible Society. Used by permission of Zondervan. All rights reserved.

Scripture quotations marked MSG are from **THE MESSAGE**. Copyright © by Eugene H. Peterson 1993, 1994, 1995, 1996, 2000, 2001, 2002. Used by permission of NavPress Publishing Group.

Published by Barbour Publishing, Inc., P.O. Box 719, Uhrichsville, Ohio 44683, www.barbourbooks.com

Our mission is to publish and distribute inspirational products offering exceptional value and biblical encouragement to the masses.

 Member of the
Evangelical Christian
Publishers Association

Printed in China.

Whispers of
Encouragement

BARBOUR

Embrace Today

Embrace the wonder and
excitement each day brings.
For tomorrow affords us
new opportunities. . .time to
experience. . .time to create. . .time
to reflect. . .time to dream.

UNKNOWN

Look Forward

Tomorrow is a new day; you shall
begin it serenely and with too high
a spirit to be encumbered with
your old nonsense. This day is all
that is good and fair. It is too dear,
with its hopes and invitations, to
waste a moment on yesterdays.

RALPH WALDO EMERSON

You Are Not Alone

Father, when troubles come, I
never have to face them alone.
Thank You for always being with
me as my refuge and strength.
When all else fails, I put my trust
in You and am never disappointed.
Amen.

God's Love Is Everywhere

What inexpressible joy for me,
to look up through the apple
blossoms and the fluttering leaves,
and to see God's love there. . .to
look beyond to the bright blue
depths of the sky, and feel they are
a canopy of blessing—the roof of
the house of my Father.

ELIZABETH RUNDELL CHARLES

Beautiful Virtue

Beauty is the mark God sets on virtue. Every natural action is graceful; every heroic act is also decent, and causes the place and the bystanders to shine.

RALPH WALDO EMERSON

Today Is a Gift

This bright, new day, complete
with 24 hours of opportunities,
choices, and attitudes comes with
a perfectly matched set of 1,440
minutes. This unique gift, this
one day, cannot be exchanged,
replaced, or refunded. Handle with
care. Make the most of it.

UNKNOWN

Mustard Seed Faith

"If you have faith as small as a
mustard seed, you can say to this
mountain, 'Move from here to
there' and it will move. Nothing
will be impossible for you."

MATTHEW 17:20–21 NIV

Acts of Caring

Too often we underestimate the
power of a touch, a smile, a kind
word, a listening ear, an honest
compliment, or the smallest acts
of caring, all of which have the
potential to turn a life around.

LEO BUSCAGLIA

Our Only Response

We are of such value to God that He came to live among us. . .and to guide us home. He will go to any length to seek us, even to being lifted high upon the cross to draw us back to Himself. We can only respond by loving God for His love.

CATHERINE OF SIENA

Daily Joys

Daily duties are daily joys, because
they are something which God
gives us to offer unto Him, to do
our very best, in acknowledgement
of His love.

EDWARD BOUVERIE PUSEY

The Sun Still Shines

Even in winter, even in the midst
of the storm, the sun is still there.
Somewhere, up above the clouds,
it still shines and warms and pulls
at the life buried deep inside the
brown branches and frozen earth.
The sun is there! Spring will come!
The clouds cannot stay forever!

GLORIA GAITHER

What We Need

What we need is not new light, but
new sight; not new paths, but new
strength to walk in the old ones;
not new duties but new wisdom
from on high to fulfill those that
are plain before us.

UNKNOWN

Live the Life You Imagined

If one advances confidently in the direction of his dreams and endeavors to live the life which he has imagined, he will meet with success unexpected in common hours. Go confidently in the direction of your dreams! Live the life you've imagined!

HENRY DAVID THOREAU

Run with Perseverance

Let us run with perseverance the race marked out for us. Let us fix our eyes on Jesus, the author and perfecter of our faith, who for the joy set before him endured the cross, scorning its shame, and sat down at the right hand of the throne of God.

HEBREWS 12:1–2 NIV

Voyage of Discovery

We are all inventors, each sailing
out on a voyage of discovery,
guided each by a private chart, of
which there is no duplicate. The
world is all gates, all opportunities.

RALPH WALDO EMERSON

Surrendered to God

It is wonderful what miracles God works in wills that are utterly surrendered to Him. He turns hard things into easy, and bitter things into sweet. It is not that He puts easy things in the place of the hard, but he actually changes the hard thing into the easy one.

HANNAH WHITALL SMITH

My Anchor Holds

And it holds, my anchor holds;
Blow your wildest then, O gale,
On my bark so small and frail,
By His grace I shall not fail,
For my anchor holds,
My anchor holds.

W. C. MARTIN

Strong Faith

As your faith is strengthened, you
will find that there is no longer the
need to have a sense of control,
that things will flow as they will,
and that you will flow with them,
to your great delight and benefit.

EMMANUEL TENEY

Reason for the Journey

We may run, walk, stumble, drive,
or fly, but let us never lose sight of
the reason for the journey or miss a
chance to see a rainbow on the way.

GLORIA GAITHER

He Will Care for You

Father, help me realize that my wants are temporary and of little importance. Let me lean against You, Lord, relaxed in the knowledge that You will care for me. Amen.

He Has Prepared a Way

"For I know the plans I have for you," declares the LORD, "plans to prosper you and not to harm you, plans to give you hope and a future. Then you will call upon me and come and pray to me, and I will listen to you."

JEREMIAH 29:11–12 NIV

Today Is Your Best Day

As God's child, today is your best
day because you are totally and
completely dependent upon Him. . . .
God is your only rock, your only
security, your only certainty, and your
only hope.

ROY LESSIN

God Is There Already

God is down in front. He is in the tomorrows. It is tomorrow that fills [us] with dread. God is there already. All the tomorrows of our life have to pass Him before they can get to us.

F. B. MEYER

Abide with God

I long for scenes
  where man has never trod;
A place where woman
  never smil'd or wept;
There to abide with
  my creator, God,
And sleep as I in childhood
  sweetly slept;
Untroubling and untroubled
  where I lie;
The grass below—
  above the vaulted sky.

JOHN CLARE

I Will Do

I am only one, but I am one. I cannot do everything, but I can do something. And that which I can do, by the grace of God, I will do.

DWIGHT L. MOODY

Here I Am

Here I am, Lord—body, heart,
and soul. Grant that with Your
love, I may be big enough to reach
the world, and small enough to be
at one with You.

MOTHER TERESA

Uncut Diamonds

Guard well your spare moments.
They are like uncut diamonds.
Discard them and their value will
never be known. Improve them
and they will become the brightest
gems in a useful life.

RALPH WALDO EMERSON

God Calls You to Hope

I pray also that the eyes of your heart may be enlightened in order that you may know the hope to which he has called you, the riches of his glorious inheritance in the saints, and his incomparably great power for us who believe.

EPHESIANS 1:18–19 NIV

React with Praise

Whenever you react with
praise and thanksgiving for an
opportunity to grow more like
Jesus in your way of reacting to
things, instead of grumbling or
feeling self-pity, you will find
that the whole situation will be
changed into a great blessing.

HANNAH HURNARD

Beauty of His Peace

Drop Thy still dews of quietness,
Till all our strivings cease;
Take from our souls
    the strain and stress,
And let our ordered lives confess
The beauty of Thy peace.

JOHN GREENLEAF WHITTIER

The Tide Will Turn

When you get into a tight place
and everything goes against you,
till it seems as though you could
not hang on a minute longer,
never give up then, for that is just
the place and time that the tide
will turn.

HARRIET BEECHER STOWE

Present Blessings

Reflect upon your present blessings
of which every man has many; not
on your past misfortunes of which
all men have some.

CHARLES DICKENS

Hold to His Teaching

To the Jews who had believed him, Jesus said, "If you hold to my teaching, you are really my disciples. Then you will know the truth, and the truth will set you free."

JOHN 8:31–32 NIV

Rewarding Joy

The marvelous richness of human
experience would lose something
of rewarding joy if there were no
limitations to overcome. The
hilltop hour would not be half so
wonderful if there were no dark
valleys to traverse.

HELEN KELLER

You Are Indispensable

Everyone has a unique role to fill
in the world and is important in
some respect. Everyone, including
and perhaps especially you, is
indispensable.

NATHANIEL HAWTHORNE

Gratitude

Lord, thank You for every blessing,
both big and small. Help me to
be more aware of the ways in
which You take care of me, so my
gratitude can continue to grow.
Amen.

Faith Illuminates the Way

Dark as my path may seem to others, I carry a magic light in my heart. Faith, the spiritual strong searchlight, illumines the way, and although sinister doubts lurk in the shadow, I walk unafraid toward the enchanted wood where the foliage is always green, where joy abides. . .in the presence of the Lord.

HELEN KELLER

God Restores

[God]. . .rekindles burned-out
lives with fresh hope, restoring
dignity and respect to their
lives—a place in the sun! For the
very structures of earth are God's;
he has laid out his operations on a
firm foundation.

1 SAMUEL 2:8–9 MSG

Look Fear in the Face

You gain strength, courage, and
confidence by every experience in
which you really stop to look fear
in the face. You must do the thing
that you think you cannot do.

ELEANOR ROOSEVELT

Ask for Grace

Grace is available for each of
us every day. . .but we've got to
remember to ask for it with a
grateful heart and not worry about
whether there will be enough for
tomorrow.

SARAH BAN BREATHNACH

Faith with Freedom

So long as faith
   with freedom reigns,
And loyal hope survives,
And gracious charity remains
To leaven lowly lives;
While there is one untrodden tract
For intellect or will,
And men are free to think and act,
Life is worth living still.

ALFRED AUSTIN

The Gift of Making Friends

Blessed are they who have the gift
of making friends, for it is one of
God's best gifts. It involves many
things, but above all the power
of going out of one's self and
appreciating what is noble and
loving in another.

Thomas Hughes

Be Available for God's Work

You simply have to be yourself—at
any age—as God made you,
available to Him so that He can
work in and through you to bring
about His kingdom and His glory.

LUCI SWINDOLL

Step out in Service

Your heart is beating with God's
love; open it to others. He has
entrusted you with gifts and
talents; use them for His service.
He goes before you each step of the
way; walk in faith. Take courage.
Step out into the unknown with
the One who knows all.

ELLYN SANNA

Forever

Forever, Lord—what
encouragement is in that word.
We have all eternity to spend with
You in heaven. Thank You for this
indescribable gift. Thank You for
being the Alpha and the Omega,
the first and the last. Amen.

The World of the Generous

The world of the generous gets
larger and larger. . . . The one
who blesses others is abundantly
blessed; those who help others are
helped.

PROVERBS 11:24–25 MSG

My Crown

My crown is in my heart,
  not on my head,
Not decked with diamonds
  and Indian stones,
Nor to be seen;
  my crown is called content;
A crown it is that seldom
  kings enjoy.

WILLIAM SHAKESPEARE, *HENRY VI*

Success in Life

If you wish success in life, make
perseverance your bosom friend,
experience your wise counselor,
caution your elder brother, and
hope your guardian genius.

JOSEPH ADDISON

Go Above and Beyond

Excellence can be attained if you care more than others think is wise, risk more than others think is safe, dream more than others think is practical, and expect more than others think is possible.

UNKNOWN

Make Others Happy

Try to make at least one person
happy every day, and then in ten
years you may have made three
thousand six hundred and fifty
persons happy, or brightened a
small town by your contribution to
the fund of general enjoyment.

SYDNEY SMITH

Love and Friendship

Human love and the delights of
friendship, out of which are built
the memories that endure, are also
to be treasured up as hints of what
shall be hereafter.

BEDE JARRETT

The Strength of Cheerfulness

Wondrous is the strength of
cheerfulness, and its power of
endurance—the cheerful man will
do more in the same time, will do
it better, will preserve it longer,
than the sad or sullen.

THOMAS CARLYLE

Those Who Wait upon God

For even young people tire and drop out, young folk in their prime stumble and fall. But those who wait upon God get fresh strength. They spread their wings and soar like eagles. They run and don't get tired, they walk and don't lag behind.

ISAIAH 40:30–31 MSG

What Waits over the Horizon

The best thing we can hope for
in this life is a knothole peek at
the shining realities ahead. Yet
a glimpse is enough. It's enough
to convince our hearts that
whatever sufferings and sorrows
currently assail us aren't worthy
of comparison to that which waits
over the horizon.

JONI EARECKSON TADA

Joy

Joy is prayer. Joy is strength. Joy is
love. Joy is a net of love by which
you can catch souls. She gives
most who gives with joy.

MOTHER TERESA

Carve Your Name on Hearts

A good character is the best tombstone. Those who loved you, and were helped by you, will remember you when the forget-me-nots are withered. Carve your name on hearts, and not on marble.

CHARLES H. SPURGEON

The Happiness of Life

The happiness of life is made up
of minute fractions—the little,
soon-forgotten charities of a
kiss or a smile, a kind look or a
heartfelt compliment.

SAMUEL TAYLOR COLERIDGE

Love Unselfishly

Instead of being unhappy, just let
your love grow as God wants it to
grow. Seek goodness in others. Love
more persons more. . .unselfishly,
without thought of return. The
return, never fear, will take care
of itself.

HENRY DRUMMOND

Instead of Worrying, Pray

Don't fret or worry. Instead of
worrying, pray. Let petitions
and praises shape your worries
into prayers, letting God know
your concerns. Before you know
it, a sense of God's wholeness,
everything coming together for
good, will come and settle you
down.

PHILIPPIANS 4:6–7 MSG

The Father's Solace

Heavenly Father, I find it hard
to find time to relax. Thank You
for making me to lie down even
when I don't want to. Thank You
for leading me beside quiet waters
when I need the solace. Amen.

Hope

Hope is not the conviction that
something will turn out well,
but the certainty that something
makes sense regardless of how it
turns out.

VÁCLAV HAVEL

Going God's Way

The strength and the happiness of
a man consists in finding out the
way in which God is going, and
going in that way, too.

HENRY WARD BEECHER

The Word of God

For the word of God is living and active. Sharper than any doubled-edged sword, it penetrates even to dividing soul and spirit, joints and marrow; it judges the thoughts and attitudes of the heart.

HEBREWS 4:12 NIV

God's Spirit Changes Us

God offers us His Spirit, not just
as an encouragement, but as a
heart-changer. He enters into us
and begins to redesign our interior
life. Suddenly our actions and
our words are truthful, kind, and
fair. No longer do they reflect the
blackness that painted our hearts,
but the rainbow of colors of His
blessings.

PAMELA MCQUADE

No Limit to His Blessings

His love has no limits,
His grace has no measure,
His power no boundary
  known unto men;
For out of His infinite riches
  in Jesus
He giveth, and giveth,
  and giveth again.

ANNIE JOHNSON FLINT

The Future Starts Now!

What a God we have! And how
fortunate we are to have him,
this Father of our Master Jesus!
Because Jesus was raised from the
dead, we've been given a brand-new
life and have everything to live for,
including a future in heaven—
and the future starts now!

1 Peter 1:3–4 msg

Be Glad of Life

Be glad of life, because it gives you
the chance to love and to work
and to play and to look up at the
stars; to be satisfied with your
possessions. . .to think seldom
of your enemies, often of your
friends, and every day of Christ;
and to spend as much time as you
can, with body and with spirit in
God's out-of-doors—these are
little guideposts on the footpath to
peace.

HENRY VAN DYKE

Be God's Kindness

Let no one ever come to you
without leaving better and happier.
Be the living expression of God's
kindness: kindness in your face,
kindness in your eyes, kindness in
your smile.

MOTHER TERESA

Keep Happy and Joyful

Joy is the holy fire that keeps our purpose warm and our intelligence aglow. Work without joy is nothing. Resolve to keep happy, and your joy and you shall form an invincible host against difficulties.

HELEN KELLER

A Sacredness in Tears

There is a sacredness in tears.
They are not the mark of
weakness, but of power. They
speak more eloquently than ten
thousand tongues. They are the
messengers of overwhelming
grief, of deep contrition, and of
unspeakable love.

WASHINGTON IRVING

How Beautiful to Be Alive

How beautiful it is to be alive!
To wake each morn
   as if the Maker's grace
Did us afresh from
   nothingness derive,
That we might sing
"How happy is our case!
How beautiful it is to be alive!"

HENRY SEPTIMUS SUTTON

I Am Your Child

Lord, I am Your child, and You delight in me whenever I fall. You pick me up, give me a hug, and encourage me to try again. Thank You for rejoicing over me.

RACHEL QUILLIN AND NANCY J. FARRIER

Hope: The Day-star of Might!

Hope floods my heart with delight!
Running on air, mad with life,
   dizzy, reeling,
Upward I mount—faith is sight,
   life is feeling,
Hope is the day-star of might!

MARGARET WITTER FULLER

The Days of Childhood

Let me play in the sunshine;
Let me sing for joy;
Let me grow in the light;
Let me splash in the rain,
And remember the days of my
childhood forever.

UNKNOWN

Wait for the Lord

I wait for the LORD, my soul waits,
and in his word I put my hope.
My soul waits for the LORD more
than watchmen wait for the
morning. . . . For with the Lord is
unfailing love and with him is full
redemption.

PSALM 130:5–7 NIV

Keep Hearts Young and Eyes Open

Half the joy of life is in little things taken on the run. Let us run if we must. . .but let us keep our hearts young and our eyes open that nothing worth our while shall escape us. And everything is worth its while if we only grasp it and its significance.

CHARLES VICTOR CHERBULIEZ

No More Fear

Lord, remove the fears that bind
me so that I can be happy in the
knowledge that You are there to
comfort me—no matter what else
is happening. Amen.

An Upward Leap of the Heart

Prayer is an upward leap of the heart, an untroubled glance toward heaven, a cry of gratitude and love which I utter from the depths of sorrow as well as from the heights of joy. It has supernatural grandeur that expands the soul and unites it with God.

THÉRÈSE OF LISIEUX

Dust in the Balance

All the joy and delight, all the
pleasures a thousand worlds could
offer, are as dust in the balance
when weighed against one hour of
this mutual exchange of love and
communion with the Lord.

CORA HARRIS MACILRAVY

Pay Praises for Blessings

The sun. . .in its full glory,
Either at rising or setting—this
And many other like blessings
   we enjoy daily;
And for the most of them,
Because they are so common,
Most men forget to
   pay their praises.
But let not us.

IZAAK WALTON

Depend upon Him

Let us begin from this moment to acknowledge Him in all our ways, and do everything, whatsoever we do, as service to Him and for His glory, depending upon Him alone for wisdom, and strength, and sweetness, and patience.

HANNAH WHITALL SMITH

Look forward with Hope

Do not look forward to the
changes and chances of this life
in fear; rather look to them with
full hope that, as they arise, God,
whose you are, will deliver you out
of them.

ST. FRANCIS DE SALES

Courage Is from the Heart

The word *courage* comes from the
Latin word for *heart*—and courage
is born in the heart. Courageous
acts come from the heart. And
a courageous life is lived from
the heart. So live your life from
your heart, and you will find the
courage you need entwined in your
living.

UNKNOWN

Another Chance

If you have made mistakes, even
serious ones, there is always
another chance for you. What we
call failure is not the falling down,
but the staying down.

MARY PICKFORD

As Others See You

My friend, if I could give you one
thing, I would wish for you the
ability to see yourself as others see
you. Then you would realize what
a truly special person you are.

B. A. BILLINGSLY

Count Flowers

When we start to count flowers,
   we cease to count weeds;
When we start to count blessings,
   we cease to count needs;
When we start to count laughter,
   we cease to count tears;
When we start to count memories,
   we cease to count years.

UNKNOWN

Sailing to Eternity

The river of Thy grace
  is flowing free;
We launch upon its depths
  to sail to Thee.
In the ocean of Thy love
  we soon shall be;
We are sailing to eternity.

PAUL RADER

Eternal Encouragement

May our Lord Jesus Christ
himself and God our Father, who
loved us and by his grace gave us
eternal encouragement and good
hope, encourage your hearts and
strengthen you in every good deed
and word.

2 THESSALONIANS 2:16–17 NIV

God's Burden

A burden, even a small one, when carried alone and in isolation can destroy us, but a burden when carried as part of God's burden can lead us to new life. That is the great mystery of our faith.

HENRI NOUWEN

Trust God

Take hours, minutes, and moments as they come, one at a time. Don't run ahead. Do what you can now. . .and at the end of the day, let it go. Put all that is left undone in God's hands. God is at work in ways you cannot see. Trust Him. Sleep. . .rest. . . Relax in His arms.

ELLYN SANNA

The Simple Things

When we take time to notice the simple things in life, we never lack for encouragement. We discover we are surrounded by limitless hope that's just wearing everyday clothes.

ANONYMOUS

The Father Guides

Father, I get discouraged when
I don't know which way to go.
Remind me that You are right
behind me, telling me which way
to turn. Help me to be quiet and
listen for your guidance. Amen.

Obey Jesus' Teaching

Jesus replied, "If anyone loves me, he will obey my teaching. My Father will love him, and we will come to him and make our home with him."

JOHN 14:23 NIV

Hope Doesn't Fail

When God holds us up, weariness
need not destroy us. We can rest in
God, then continue on with a firm
step. Through prayer and scripture,
refreshment comes, along with a
new sense of purpose. Hope does
not fail when it's put in the Savior.

PAMELA MCQUADE

Bound to Be True

I am not bound to win, but I am
bound to be true. I am not bound
to succeed, but I am bound to live
by the light that I have. I must
stand with anybody that stands
right, stand with him while he is
right, and part [company] with him
when he goes wrong.

ABRAHAM LINCOLN

Unique Creation

The way you are put together
is unique—different from any
other. Even identical twins can
be distinguished by voice or
mannerisms. God has designed
you wonderfully well. He thinks
about you every minute of every
day. He has a special purpose just
for you, a niche that only you can
fill.

LORI SHANKLE

Live Full Lives

Live full lives, full in the fullness
of God. God can do anything, you
know—far more than you could
ever imagine or guess or request
in your wildest dreams! He does
it not by pushing us around but
by working within us, his Spirit
deeply and gently within us.

EPHESIANS 3:19–20 MSG

A Bigger Picture

There is something satisfying,
rejuvenating, comforting about
the seasons. They remind me that
I play one small part in a much
bigger picture—that there is a
pulse, a sequence, a journey set
into motion by the very hand of
God Himself.

KAREN SCALF LINAMEN

Where He Delights to Dwell

All God's glory and beauty come
from within, and there He delights
to dwell. His visits there are
frequent, His conversation sweet,
His comforts refreshing, His peace
passing all understanding.

THOMAS À KEMPIS

Open Wide

Open wide the windows of our
spirits and fill us full of light; open
wide the door of our hearts, that
we may receive and entertain Thee
with all our powers of adoration.

CHRISTINA ROSSETTI

A Bright Torch

Life is no brief candle to me. It is a sort of splendid torch which I have got a hold of for the moment, and I want to make it burn as brightly as possible before handing it on to future generations.

GEORGE BERNARD SHAW

Kind Words

Kind words produce their own image
in men's souls; and a beautiful image
it is. They soothe and quiet and
comfort the hearer. . . . We have not
yet begun to use kind words in such
abundance as they ought to be used.

BLAISE PASCAL

The Good Shepherd

Father, Your guidance is
trustworthy. You are our Good
Shepherd. You lead us to places of
rest when we need them. Thank
You for Your leading. Amen.

God Gives Endurance and Encouragement

For everything that was written in the past was written to teach us, so that through endurance and the encouragement of the Scriptures we might have hope. May the God who gives endurance and encouragement give you a spirit of unity among yourselves.

ROMANS 15:4–5 NIV

Nurture the Spirit of Stillness

Do whatever is necessary to
nurture the spirit of stillness in
your life. Don't let the enemy wear
you so thin that you lose your
balance and perspective. Regular
time for stillness is as important
and necessary as sleep, exercise,
and nutritional food.

EMILIE BARNES

Shining Through

As a countenance is made
beautiful by the soul's shining
through it, so the world is
beautiful by the shining through it
of God.

FRIEDRICH HEINRICH JACOBI

Appreciate the Beauty and Wonder

I find each day too short for all the
thoughts I want to think, all the
walks I want to take, all the books
I want to read, and all the friends
I want to see. The longer I live,
the more my mind dwells upon
the beauty and the wonder of the
world.

JOHN BURROUGHS

As I Am

Grace means God accepts
me just as I am. He does not
require or insist that I measure
up to someone else's standard
of performance. He loves me
completely, thoroughly, and
perfectly. There is nothing I can
do to add to or detract from that
love.

MARY GRAHAM

Unutterable Fulfillment

Occasionally in my life there are those moments of unutterable fulfillment which cannot be completely explained by those symbols called words. Their meanings can only be articulated by the inaudible language of the heart.

MARTIN LUTHER KING JR.

The Lord Will Be Your Confidence

Have no fear of sudden disaster
or of the ruin that overtakes the
wicked, for the LORD will be your
confidence and will keep your foot
from being snared.

PROVERBS 3:25–26 NIV

Leave a Hopeful Impulse

Every heart that has beat strong
and cheerfully has left a hopeful
impulse behind it in the world and
bettered the tradition of mankind.

ROBERT LOUIS STEVENSON

Shine on Others

Dear Lord. . .shine through me,
and be so in me that every soul
I come in contact with may feel
Your presence in my soul. . . . Let
me thus praise You in the way
You love best, by shining on those
around me.

JOHN HENRY NEWMAN

A Still, Small Voice

There is a voice, "a still,
   small voice" of love,
Heard from above;
But not amidst the din
   of earthly sounds,
Which here confounds;
By those withdrawn apart
   it best is heard,
And peace, sweet peace
Breathes in each gentle word.

UNKNOWN

Discover the Good News!

Everyone has inside of him a piece
of good news. The good news is
that you don't know how great you
can be! How much you can love!
What you can accomplish! And
what your potential is!

ANNE FRANK

A Thankful Spirit

Make it a rule to yourself to thank
and praise God for everything that
happens to you. For it is certain
that whatever seeming calamity
happens to you, if you thank and
praise God for it, you turn it into
a blessing. Could you, therefore,
work miracles, you could not do
more for yourself than by this
thankful spirit; for it heals with a
word speaking and turns all that it
touches into happiness.

WILLIAM LAW

Keep Moving in the Right Direction

I find the great thing in this world
is not so much where we stand, as
in what direction we are moving.
To reach the port of heaven, we
must sail sometimes with the wind
and sometimes against it—but we
must sail, and not drift, nor lie at
anchor.

OLIVER WENDELL HOLMES

God Promises Life without End

My aim is to raise hopes by
pointing the way to life without
end. This is the life God promised
long ago—and he doesn't break
promises!

TITUS 1:2 MSG

God Is Everywhere

There's not a tint
 that paints the rose
Or decks the lily fair,
Or marks the humblest
 flower that grows,
But God has placed it there. . . .
There's not a place
 on earth's vast round,
In ocean's deep or air,
Where love and beauty
 are not found,
For God is everywhere.

UNKNOWN

Trust Him

Trust Him when dark doubts
   assail thee.
Trust Him when thy
   strength is small.
Trust Him when to
   simply trust Him
Seems the hardest thing of all.
Trust Him, He is ever faithful;
Trust Him, for He is the best;
Trust Him, for the heart of Jesus
Is the only place of rest.

SALESIAN MISSIONS

He Made and Loveth All

Speak, Lord, for
   Thy servant heareth;
Speak peace to my anxious soul,
And help me to feel
   that all my ways
Are under Thy wise control;
The He who cares for the lily,
And heeds the sparrows' fall,
Shall tenderly lead
   His loving child:
For He made and loveth all.

UNKNOWN

The Spirit of Love

You will find, as you look back
upon your life, that the moments
when you have really lived are the
moments when you have done
things in the spirit of love.

HENRY DRUMMOND

Praise, Don't Complain

There is no mistaking, Lord.
You've made it clear that I'm to be
joyful in each and every task. The
next time I'm tempted to complain
about the mounds of work, remind
me to turn the murmuring into
praise. Amen.

Give Happiness

Whether any particular day shall
bring to you more of happiness
or of suffering is largely beyond
your power to determine. Whether
each day of your life shall give
happiness or suffering rests within
yourself.

GEORGE S. MERRIAM

Confidence in God

I place no hope in my strength,
nor in my works: but all my
confidence is in God my protector,
who never abandons those who
have put all their hope and
thought in Him.

FRANÇOIS RABELAIS

Every Task Matters

I long to accomplish great and
noble tasks, but it is my chief duty
to accomplish humble tasks as
though they were great and noble.
The world is moved along not only
by the mighty shoves of its heroes,
but also by the aggregate of the
tiny pushes of each honest worker.

HELEN KELLER

Go out in Joy

You will go out in joy and be led
forth in peace; the mountains and
hills will burst into song before
you, and all the trees of the field
will clap their hands.

Isaiah 55:12 niv

May Jesus Christ Be Praised!

When morning guilds the skies, my heart awakening cries: May Jesus Christ be praised! Alike at work and prayer, to Jesus I repair: May Jesus Christ be praised!

JOSEPH BARNBY

A Kind Father

God is a kind Father. He sets us all
in the places where He wishes us to
be employed; and that employment
is truly "our Father's business." He
chooses work for every creature. . . .
He gives us always strength enough,
and sense enough, for what He
wants us to do.

JOHN RUSKIN

The Light of Love, Faith, and Hope

In the dark dreary nights, when
the storm is at its most fierce, the
lighthouse burns bright so the
sailors can find their way home
again. In life the same light burns.
This light is fueled with love, faith,
and hope. And through life's most
fierce storms these three burn
their brightest so we also can find
our way home again.

UNKNOWN

He Designed You

Your identity is the result of
neither coincidence nor accident.
You are who you are because of
God's loving design. He wanted
you to be *you*, and no one else.

DARLENE SALA

Your Face Upturned

Bask in the sunshine of [God's] love. Drink of the waters of His goodness. Keep your face upturned to Him as the flowers do to the sun. Look, and your soul shall live and grow.

HANNAH WHITALL SMITH

Unchangeable Beauty

The beauty of the earth, the beauty
of the sky, the order of the stars,
the sun, the moon. . .their very
loveliness is their confession of
God: for who made these lovely
mutable things, but He who is
Himself unchangeable beauty?

AUGUSTINE

Turn It into a Blessing

If anyone would tell you the shortest, surest way to happiness and all perfection, he must tell you to make it a rule to yourself to thank and praise God for everything that happens to you. For it is certain that whatever seeming calamity happens to you, if you thank and praise God for it, you turn it into a blessing.

UNKNOWN

Come Forth as Gold

We will all "come forth as gold"
if we understand that God is
sovereign and knows what is best,
even when we cannot understand
what is happening at the time. He
asks us to trust Him and to know
that He cares for us even when we
can't track Him.

SHIRLEY DOBSON

His Unfailing Love

How priceless is your unfailing love! Both high and low among men find refuge in the shadow of your wings. They feast on the abundance of your house; you give them drink from your river of delights. For with you is the fountain of life; in your light we see light.

PSALM 36:7–9 NIV

The Wonder of Living

The wonder of living is held
within the beauty of silence, the
glory of sunlight, the sweetness of
fresh spring air, the quiet strength
of earth, and the love that lies at
the very root of all things.

ANONYMOUS

From Miracle to Miracle

To be alive, to be able to see, to
walk, to have a home. . .it's all
a miracle. I have adopted the
technique of living life from
miracle to miracle.

ARTHUR RUBENSTEIN

Footprints on Your Soul

Life is full of people who will make you laugh, cry, smile until your face hurts, and so happy that you think you'll burst. But the ones who leave their footprints on your soul are the ones that keep your life going.

NATALIE BERNOT

Rejoice in Him

Father, praising You and rejoicing
in You must be high on my priority
list. Proclaiming Your love to
others must never be lacking in my
life. Thank You that I am able to
rejoice in You! Amen.

Joy Without and Joy Within

To be a joy-bearer and a joy-giver
says everything, for in our life, if
one is joyful, it means that one is
faithfully living for God, and that
nothing else counts; and if one
gives joy to others, one is doing
God's work; with joy without and
joy within, all is well.

JANET ERSKINE STUART

A New Song

He lifted me out of the slimy pit,
out of the mud and mire; he set my
feet on a rock and gave me a firm
place to stand. He put a new song
in my mouth, a hymn of praise to
our God.

PSALM 40:2–3 NIV

The Streams of Living Waters

See, the streams of living waters,
Springing from eternal love,
Well supply thy sons and daughters
And all fear of want remove:
Who can faint while such a river
Ever flows their thirst to assuage?
Grace which, like the Lord,
 the Giver,
Never fails from age to age.

JOHN NEWTON

Thank You, Lord

Thank You, Lord, for Your love
and faithfulness to us. Thank You
for making us Your people, for
allowing us to be the sheep of Your
pasture. Thank You for allowing us
to serve such a great God! Amen.

Believe

Faith is the root of all blessings.
Believe and you shall be saved;
believe and your needs must be
satisfied; believe and you cannot
but be comforted and happy.

JEREMY TAYLOR

Most Amazing Day

I thank You, God, for this most
amazing day, for the leaping
greenly spirits of trees, and for
the blue dream of sky and for
everything which is natural, which
is infinite, which is yes.

E. E CUMMINGS

The Focus of His Love

How blessed is God! And what a blessing he is! He's the Father of our Master, Jesus Christ, and takes us to the high places of blessing in him. Long before he laid down earth's foundations, he had us in mind, had settled on us as the focus of his love.

EPHESIANS 1:3–4 MSG

An Angel's Song

Kind words are the music of the
world. They have a power which
seems to be beyond natural causes,
as if they were some angel's song
which had lost its way and come
on earth.

FREDERICK WILLIAM FABER

No Cause of Fear

If the Lord be with us, we have no
cause of fear. His eye is upon us,
His arm over us, His ear open to
our prayer—His grace sufficient,
His promise unchangeable.

JOHN NEWTON

Make the Lights Prevail

An optimist is a person who sees
only the lights in the picture,
whereas a pessimist sees only the
shadows. An idealist, however,
is one who sees the light and the
shadows, but in addition sees
something else: the possibility of
changing the picture, of making
the lights prevail over the shadows.

FELIX ADLER

Pure and Lovely

The things we think on are the things that feed our souls. If we think on pure and lovely things, we shall grow pure and lovely like them.

HANNAH WHITALL SMITH

Guide and Cheer Others

Our gifts and attainments are not
only to be light and warmth in
our own dwellings, but are also to
shine through the windows into
the dark night, to guide and cheer
bewildered travelers on the road.

HENRY WARD BEECHER

Get Some Distance

Every now and then go away,
have a little relaxation, for when
you come back to your work your
judgment will be surer. Go some
distance away because then the
work appears smaller and more of
it can be taken in at a glance.

LEONARDO DA VINCI

My Reward Awaits Me

Father, my daily problems come
and go; yet if I remain steadfast
and dedicated, doing the work
You have given me to do, I am
confident that my reward awaits
me. Thank You, Lord. Amen.

Keep Thou Thy Dreams

Keep thou thy dreams—
The tissue of all wings
Is woven first of them;
From dreams are made
The precious and
    imperishable things
Whose loveliness lives on
    and does not fade.

VIRNA SHEARD

True Success

To appreciate beauty; to find the best in others; to give one's self; to leave the world a little better, whether by a healthy child, a garden patch, or a redeemed social condition; to have played and laughed with enthusiasm, and sung with exultation; to know even one life has breathed easier because you have lived. . .this is to have succeeded.

RALPH WALDO EMERSON

Christ Dwells within Me

I know Christ dwells within me
all the time, guiding me and
inspiring me whenever I do or
say anything—a light of which I
caught no glimmer before it comes
to me at the very moment when it
is needed.

St. Therese of Lisieux

The Lord Is the Everlasting God

Why do you say. . ."My way is hidden from the LORD; my cause is disregarded by my God"? Do you not know? Have you not heard? The LORD is the everlasting God, the Creator of the ends of the earth. He will not grow tired or weary, and his understanding no one can fathom.

ISAIAH 40:27–28 NIV

Our Hearts Are His

If we believe in Jesus, we've been cast a lifeline. We've connected ourselves to Him in faith, and though we struggle to work out our beliefs with consistency, our hearts are truly His. That internal confidence earned us the greatest reward: eternity with our Savior.

PAMELA MCQUADE

Like Embroidery

Take your needle, my child,
and work at your pattern; it will
come out a rose by and by. Life
is like that; one stitch at a time
taken patiently, and the pattern
will come out all right, like
embroidery.

OLIVER WENDELL HOLMES

Every Flower

The splendor of the rose and the
whiteness of the lily do not rob
the little violet of its scent nor the
daisy of its simple charm. If every
tiny flower wanted to be a rose,
spring would lose its loveliness.

ST. THERESE OF LISIEUX

His Infinity and Simplicity

God is infinite in His simplicity
and simple in His infinity.
Therefore He is everywhere
and is everywhere complete.
He is everywhere on account of
His infinity, and is everywhere
complete on account of His
simplicity.

MEISTER ECKHART

Look to This Day!

Look to this day! For it is life,
the very life of life. For yesterday
is but a dream, and tomorrow is
only a vision, but today well lived
makes every yesterday a dream of
happiness and tomorrow a vision
of hope.

KALIDASA

Rewards of the Simple Life

To find the universal elements
enough; to find the air and the
water exhilarating; to be refreshed
by a morning walk or an evening
saunter. . .to be thrilled by the
stars at night; to be elated over
a bird's nest or a wildflower in
spring—these are some of the
rewards of the simple life.

JOHN BURROUGHS

The World Is Full of Beauty

There is beauty in the forest
When the trees are green and fair;
There is beauty in the meadow
When the wildflowers scent the air.
There is beauty in the sunlight
And the soft blue beams above.
Oh, the world is full of beauty
When the heart is full of love.

UNKNOWN

His Everlasting Way

By following Jesus, you always
head in the right direction.
Though the way may seem dark
or convoluted, and you may often
wonder if you're on the right track,
as His Spirit leads you, you cannot
go wrong. Your powerful Lord
directs you in His everlasting way.

PAMELA MCQUADE

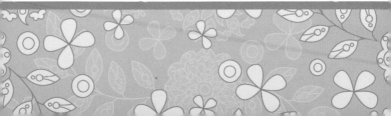

His Compassions Never Fail

This I call to mind and therefore
I have hope: Because of the LORD's
great love we are not consumed,
for his compassions never fail.
They are new every morning; great
is your faithfulness.

LAMENTATIONS 3:21–23 NIV

May Grace Leap Out at You

My prayer is that God will surprise
you today. In your daily routine,
in the stressful details of ordinary
life, when you least expect it, may
grace leap out at you, encouraging
your heart.

ELLYN SANNA

Prayers Are Answered

Lord, when I see how You have interceded on my behalf, I want to fall on my face before You. My prayers have been answered in miraculous ways. In times when all I could see was darkness, You provided light and power and hope. Amen.

Be Better

Always dream and shoot higher
than you know how to. Don't
bother just to be better than your
contemporaries or predecessors.
Try to be better than yourself.

WILLIAM FAULKNER

Follow Aspirations

Far away there in the sunshine are
my highest aspirations.
I may not reach them, but I can
look up and see their beauty,
Believe in them, and try to follow
where they lead.

LOUISA MAY ALCOTT

An Instrument of Thy Peace

Lord, make me an instrument of Thy peace. Where there is hatred, let me sow love. Where there is injury, pardon. Where there is doubt, faith. Where there is despair, hope. Where there is darkness, light. Where there is sadness, joy.

ST. FRANCIS OF ASSISI

Tremendous Treasure in Nature

If we are children of God, we have
a tremendous treasure in nature
and will realize that it is holy and
sacred. We will see God reaching
out to us in every wind that blows,
every sunrise and sunset, every
cloud in the sky, every flower that
blooms, and every leaf that fades.

OSWALD CHAMBERS

My Strength and My Shield

The LORD is my strength and my
shield; my heart trusts in him, and
I am helped. My heart leaps for joy
and I will give thanks to him in
song.

PSALM 28:7 NIV

Peace at Last

May He support us all the day long, till the shades lengthen, and the evening comes, and the busy world is hushed, and the fever of life is over, and our work is done! Then in His mercy may He give us a safe lodging and a holy rest, and peace at last.

JOHN HENRY CARDINAL NEWMAN

In Your Peace

Calm me, O Lord,
  as you stilled the storm,
Still me, O Lord,
  keep me from harm.
Let all the tumult within me cease,
Enfold me, Lord, in Your peace.

CELTIC TRADITIONAL

Every Step

When we are facing dire troubles, God never deserts us. As life ebbs away, He does not step back from our need. No, the Eternal One guides us every step of the way, whether life is joyous or discouraging. God never gives up on you and never fails you. So don't give up on yourself.

PAMELA MCQUADE

A Wilderness of Blossom

I know nothing so pleasant as to sit there on a summer afternoon, with the western sun flickering through the great elder-tree. . .where flowers and flowering shrubs are set as thick as grass in a field, a wilderness of blossom, interwoven, intertwined, wreathy, garland, profuse beyond all profusion.

MARY MITFORD

No Situation Too Chaotic

There is no situation so chaotic that God cannot, from that situation, create something that is surpassingly good. He did it at the creation. He did it at the cross. He is doing it today.

BISHOP MOULE

Brim Over

Oh! May the God of green hope
fill you up with joy, fill you up with
peace, so that your believing lives,
filled with the life-giving energy
of the Holy Spirit, will brim over
with hope!

ROMANS 15:13 MSG

My Heart

My heart is like a singing bird
Whose nest is in a water'd shoot;
My heart is like an apple-tree
Whose boughs are bent
  with thick-set fruit;
My heart is like a rainbow shell
That paddles in a halcyon sea;
My heart is gladder than all these,
Because my love is come to me.

CHRISTINA ROSSETTI

Become as Little Children

Take time for make-believe.
Abandon yourself in play. I think
God gives us an imagination
for a reason. Christ knows the
pressures we endure. Perhaps this
is one reason He encourages us to
"become as little children."

JEAN LUSH WITH PAM VREDEVELT

On the Right Path

Thank You for Your promise to
preserve me if I love You, Father.
I know that this is an eternal
promise. What more incentive do
I need to pursue a right walk with
You? Keep me on the right path,
Lord. Amen.

The Shepherd Guides

Left to our own agendas, we either
run at breakneck speeds right past
the pasture. . .or sit in the parched
desert. The Shepherd. . .intervenes
on our behalf to guide us. . .onto a
quiet path and into a calmer faith.

PATSY CLAIRMONT

Life Is What We Are Alive To

Life is what we are alive to. It is
not length but breadth. . . . Be
alive to. . .goodness, kindness,
purity, love, history, poetry, music,
flowers, stars, God, and eternal
hope.

MALTBIE D. BABCOCK

God Has Promised

The same God who guides the
stars in their courses, who directs
the earth in its orbit, who feeds
the burning furnace of the sun
and keeps the stars perpetually
burning with their fires—the same
God has promised to supply thy
strength.

CHARLES H. SPURGEON

Never Lose an Opportunity

Never lose an opportunity
of seeing anything that is
beautiful; for beauty is God's
handwriting—a wayside
sacrament. Welcome it in every
fair face, in every fair sky, in every
fair flower, and thank God for it as
a cup of blessing.

RALPH WALDO EMERSON

Opportunities of a Richer Service

It may be one more request than
we think we can fulfill, one more
responsibility that we think we can
manage. . . . Interruptions never
distracted Jesus. He accepted them
as opportunities of a richer service.

RUTH BELL GRAHAM

His Promise Is Unchangeable

God can't break his word.
And because his word cannot
change, the promise is likewise
unchangeable. We who have run
for our very lives to God have
every reason to grab the promised
hope with both hands and never
let go.

HEBREWS 6:18 MSG

A Friend Encourages

We occasionally have moments
when we're perfectly content
to feel gloomy. . . . Then along
comes a friend who manages to
encourage a smile, and if she tries
really hard, can even send you into
a fit of laughter.

ANITA WIEGAND

God's Grace

God's grace is too big, too great
to understand fully. So we must
take the moments of His grace
throughout the day with us: the
music of the songbird in the
morning, the kindness shown in
the afternoon, and the restful
sleep at night.

ANONYMOUS

Faith Arms from Fear

No coward soul is mine,
No trembler in the world's
 storm-troubled sphere:
I see heaven's glories shine,
And faith shines equal,
 arming me from fear.

EMILY BRONTË

The Sweetest Things in Life

The best things in life are nearest: breath in your nostrils, light in your eyes, flowers at your feet, duties at your hand, the path of right just before you. Do not grasp at the stars, but do life's plain common work as it comes, certain that daily duties and daily bread are the sweetest things in life.

ROBERT LOUIS STEVENSON

Our Journey

In such a beautiful wilderness of
wildflowers we are amused with
the very variety and novelty of
the scene so much that we in our
pleasure lose all sense of weariness
or fatigue in the length of our
wandering and get to the end
before we are aware of our journey.

JOHN CLARE

Through Faith in Christ Jesus

We must not sit still and look for miracles; up and doing, and the Lord will be with thee. Prayer and pains, through faith in Christ Jesus, will do anything.

GEORGE ELIOT

The Love of Christ

I pray that out of his glorious
riches he may strengthen you with
power through his Spirit in your
inner being, so that Christ may
dwell in your hearts through faith.
And I pray that you, being rooted
and established in love, may have
power. . .to grasp how wide and
long and high and deep is the love
of Christ.

EPHESIANS 3:16–18 NIV

New-Created

And if tonight my soul may find
her peace in sleep, and sink in
good oblivion, and in the morning
wake like a new-opened flower,
then I have been dipped again in
God, and new-created.

D. H. LAWRENCE

He Calms

Father, I can't begin to count the number of times You've wrapped Your loving arms around me and calmed me in the midst of fears. You've drawn me near in times of sorrow and given me assurance when I've faced great disappointment. Amen.

All Your Heart Might Desire

May you always have walls for
the winds, a roof for the rain, tea
beside the fire, laughter to cheer
you, those you love near you, and
all your heart might desire.

IRISH BLESSING

Knowing That She Hath Wings

Be like the bird that,
   halting in its flight
Awhile on boughs too slight
Feels them give way beneath her,
   and yet sings
Knowing that she hath wings.

VICTOR HUGO

The Hand of God

Nothing touches my life that
hasn't first passed through the
hand of God. He knows what is
best for me. I will trust His hand
in my life, believing that He sees
how all things work together.

UNKNOWN

All Delightful Conditions

Cherish your visions; cherish your
ideals; cherish the music that
stirs in your heart, the beauty that
forms in your mind, the loveliness
that drapes your purest thoughts,
for out of them will grow all
delightful conditions, all heavenly
environment.

JAMES ALLEN

Rest for Your Souls

"Come to me, all you who are weary and burdened, and I will give you rest. Take my yoke upon you and learn from me, for I am gentle and humble in heart, and you will find rest for your souls. For my yoke is easy and my burden is light."

MATTHEW 11:28–30 NIV

God Is Awake

Have courage for the great
sorrows of life and patience for
the small ones; and when you have
laboriously accomplished your
daily task, go to sleep in peace.
God is awake.

VICTOR HUGO

Continually Filled with Praise and Thanksgiving

Lord, I want my heart to continually be filled with praise and thanksgiving to You. Keep me anchored in the thought that all You do is for my good and glory. Only You are deserving of my praise and adoration. Amen.

Ideals Are Like Stars

Ideals are like stars; you will not succeed in touching them with your hands. But like the seafaring man on the desert of waters, you choose them as your guides, and following them you will reach your destiny.

CARL SCHURZ

Work for Your Hands

May there always be work for your hands to do, may your purse always hold a coin or two. May the sun always shine on your windowpane, may a rainbow be certain to follow each rain. May the hand of a friend always be near you, may God fill your heart with gladness to cheer you.

IRISH BLESSING

Put Love into Action

Love cannot remain by itself—it
has no meaning. Love has to be
put into action, and that action
is service. Whatever form we are,
able or disabled, rich or poor, it
is not how much we do, but how
much love we put in the doing;
a lifelong sharing of love with
others.

MOTHER TERESA

Heaven Breaking Through

All that is sweet, delightful, and
amiable in this world, in the
serenity of the air, the fineness
of seasons, the joy of light, the
melody of sounds, the beauty of
colors, the fragrance of smells,
the splendor of precious stones, is
nothing else but heaven breaking
through the veil of this world.

WILLIAM LAW

He Supplies

Now he who supplies seed to the sower and bread for food will also supply and increase your store of seed and will enlarge the harvest of your righteousness. You will be made rich in every way so that you can be generous on every occasion, and. . .your generosity will result in thanksgiving to God.

2 CORINTHIANS 9:10–11 NIV

I Shall Not Live in Vain

If I can stop one heart
   from breaking,
I shall not live in vain;
If I can ease one life in the aching,
Or cool one pain,
Or help one fainting robin
Unto his nest again,
I shall not live in vain.

EMILY DICKINSON

In Every Human Being's Heart

Whether sixty or sixteen, there
is in every human being's heart
the lure of wonder, the unfailing
childlike appetite of what's next,
and the joy of the game of living.

SAMUEL ULLMAN

He is Close Enough

We do not need to search for
heaven, over here or over there, in
order to find our eternal Father. In
fact, we do not even need to speak
out loud, for though we speak
in the smallest whisper or the
most fleeting thought, He is close
enough to hear us.

TERESA OF AVILA

My Hope

Lord, You are my hope in an
often hopeless world. You are
my hope of heaven, my hope
of peace, my hope of change,
purpose, and unconditional love.
Fill the reservoir of my heart to
overflowing with the joy that real
hope brings. Amen.

Little Pockets of Happiness

Between the house and the
store there are little pockets of
happiness. A bird, a garden, a
friend's greeting, a child's smile,
a cat in the sunshine needing a
stroke. Recognize them or ignore
them. It's always up to you.

PAM BROWN

Look Around—See Christ

Look backward—
  see Christ dying for you.
Look upward—
  see Christ pleading for you.
Look inward—
  see Christ living in you.
Look forward—
  see Christ coming for you.

UNKNOWN

Abundant Life

Abundant life, full of good
things on this earth, spiritual
peace and joy, and full, satisfying
relationships—that's what God
intends His people to have.
Because Jesus entered your life,
you've entered a new realm. Life
has taken on a new meaning,
because you know the Creator.

PAMELA MCQUADE

Meant to Be Immortal

Our Creator would never have
made such lovely days, and have
given us the deep hearts to enjoy
them, above and beyond all
thought, unless we were meant to
be immortal.

NATHANIEL HAWTHORNE

The Soul Is a Temple

The soul is a temple, and God
is silently building it by night
and by day. Precious thoughts
are building it, unselfish love is
building it, all-penetrating faith is
building it.

HENRY WARD BEECHER

The Path of Peace

Through the heartfelt mercies of
our God, God's Sunrise will break
in upon us, shining on those in
the darkness, those sitting in the
shadow of death, then showing us
the way, one foot at a time, down
the path of peace.

LUKE 1:78–79 MSG

It Is Well with My Soul

And Lord, haste the day
    when my faith shall be sight,
The clouds be rolled back
    as a scroll;
The trump shall resound,
    and the Lord shall descend,
Even so, it is well with my soul.

HORATIO G. SPAFFORD

God Knows

You do not know what you are
going to do; the only thing you
know is that God knows what He
is doing. . . . It is this attitude that
keeps you in perpetual wonder—
you do not know what God is
going to do next.

OSWALD CHAMBERS

A Cheerful Temper Joined with Innocence

A cheerful temper joined with innocence will make beauty attractive, knowledge delightful, and wit good-natured. It will lighten sickness, poverty, and affliction; convert ignorance into amiable simplicity, and render deformity itself agreeable.

JOSEPH ADDISON

Press On

A new life begins for us with every second. Let us go forward joyously to meet it. We must press on, whether we will or no, and we shall walk better with our eyes before us than with them ever cast behind.

UNKNOWN

The Love of God
Shine Forth from You

Let Jesus be in your heart,
Eternity in your spirit,
The world under your feet,
The will of God in your actions.
And let the love of God shine
forth from you.

CATHERINE OF GENOA

A Radiance of Thine

Help me to spread my fragrance
everywhere I go. Flood my soul
with Thy spirit and life. Penetrate
and possess my whole being so
utterly that all my life may only be
a radiance of Thine.

John Henry Cardinal Newman

Nothing to Worry About

Father, as long as I trust in Your
presence, I have nothing to worry
about. Nothing can separate me
from You, because you are the
strong protector, the mighty One
who watches over me always.
I praise You, Lord, for Your
protection. Amen.

Bathed in Sunlight

If you are generous with the
hungry and start giving yourselves
to the down-and-out, your lives
will begin to glow in the darkness,
your shadowed lives will be bathed
in sunlight.

ISAIAH 58:10 MSG

Wishes

I wish you sunshine on your path
and storms to season your journey.
I wish you peace—in the world in
which you live and in the smallest
corner of the heart where truth
is kept. I wish you faith—to help
define your living and your life.
More I cannot wish you—except
perhaps love—to make all the rest
worthwhile.

ROBERT A. WARD

Don't Linger

Treasure your memories today—
but don't linger in the past,
mourning for the "good old days."
God's presence was with you
each moment of those days, and
I know He will fill your life with
blessings—but He is also with you
today. And he has a storehouse of
blessing He still waits to give you
in the future.

ELLYN SANNA

A Balance

The best and safest thing is
to keep a balance in your life,
acknowledge the great power
around us and in us. If you can
do that, and live that way, you are
really a wise man.

EURIPIDES

Jesus

God will never, never, never let
us down if we have faith and put
our trust in Him. He will always
look after us. So we must cleave to
Jesus. Our whole life must simply
be woven into Jesus.

MOTHER TERESA

His Hand

He hideth my soul in
  the cleft of the rock
That shadows a dry, thirsty land;
He hideth my life with
  the depths of His love,
And covers me there
  with His hand,
And covers me there
  with His hand.

FANNY CROSBY

Confidence

Such confidence as this is ours
through Christ before God. Not
that we are competent in ourselves
to claim anything for ourselves, but
our competence comes from God.

2 CORINTHIANS 3:4–5 NIV

What Love Looks Like

What does [love] look like? It
has hands to help others, feet to
hasten to the poor and needy, eyes
to see misery and want, ears to
hear the sighs and sorrows of men.
That is what love looks like.

ST. AUGUSTINE

His Constant Care

Father, I praise You for Your
support. When my strength fails,
Yours is always sufficient. Thank
You for Your constant love and
care, for picking out my cry and
never failing to rescue me. Amen.

You Can Give

How lovely to think that no one
need wait a moment, we can start
now, start slowly changing the
world! How lovely that everyone,
great and small, can make their
contribution toward introducing
justice straightaway. . . . And you
can always, always give something,
even if it is only kindness!

ANNE FRANK

Believe

When you come to the edge of all
the light you have, and you must
take a step into the darkness of the
unknown, believe that one of two
things will happen. Either there
will be something solid for you to
stand on—or you will be taught
how to fly.

PATRICK OVERTON

We Thank the Keeper

For sunlit hours and visions clear,
For all remembered faces dear,
For comrades of a single day,
Who sent us stronger on our way,
For friends who shared
  the year's long road,
And bore with us the
  common load, . . .
For insights won through
  toils and tears,
We thank the Keeper of our years.

CLYDE MCGEE

Champions

Champions do not become
champions when they win the
event, but in the hours, weeks,
months, and years they spend
preparing for it. The victorious
performance itself is merely
the demonstration of their
championship character.

T. ALAN ARMSTRONG

For God So Loved

"For God so loved the world that
he gave his one and only Son, that
whoever believes in him shall not
perish but have eternal life. For
God did not send his Son into the
world to condemn the world, but
to save the world through him."

John 3:16–17 niv

Another Day

The wonderful thing about sunset,
and much the same can be said
for sunrise, is that it happens
every day, and even if the sunset
itself is not spectacular, it marks
the beginning of another day. It's
a great time to pause and take
notice.

ELAINE ST. JAMES

Reflection

Reflection. . .enables our minds to be stretched in three different directions—the direction that leads to a proper relationship with God, the relationship that leads to a healthy relationship with others, and the relationship that leads to a deeper understanding of oneself.

MARK CONNOLLY

Lift Them

We look at our burdens and heavy
loads and shrink from them; but
as we lift them and bind them with
our hearts, they become wings; and
on them we rise and soar toward
God.

MRS. CHARLES E. COWMAN

Accomplishment

Look at a day when you are
supremely satisfied at the end. It is
not a day when you lounge around
doing nothing; it is when you have
had everything to do, and you have
done it.

MARGARET THATCHER

Your Strength

Because of Your strength, Lord, I
can smile. When I need peace, You
strengthen me on the inside. This
is where I need You the most. Let
me reflect Your strength so that
others will be drawn to You, too.
Amen.

Full Life

Life is full of beauty. Notice it.
Notice the bumblebee, the small
child, and the smiling faces. Smell
the rain, and feel the wind. Live
your life to the fullest potential,
and fight for your dreams.

ASHLEY SMITH

The Beautiful

A person should hear a little music, read a little poetry, and see a fine picture every day of their life, in order that worldly cares may not obliterate the sense of the beautiful which God has implanted in the human soul.

JOHANN WOLFGANG VON GOETHE

Attitude

Your living is determined not so
much by what life brings to you as
by the attitude you bring to life;
not so much by what happens to
you as by the way your mind looks
at what happens.

KAHLIL GIBRAN

Work Hard

Are you bored with life? Then
throw yourself into some work you
believe in with all your heart, live
for it, die for it, and you will find
happiness that you had thought
could never be yours.

DALE CARNEGIE

With All Your Heart

Whatever you do, work at it with all your heart, as working for the Lord, not for men, since you know that you will receive an inheritance from the Lord as a reward. It is the Lord Christ you are serving.

COLOSSIANS 3:23–24 NIV

A Friend

So long as we love, we serve;
so long as we are loved by
others, I would say that we are
indispensable; and no man is
useless while he has a friend.

ROBERT LOUIS STEVENSON

Be Wholly Alive

Try as much as possible to be
wholly alive, with all your might,
and when you laugh, laugh like
hell and when you get angry, get
good and angry. Try to be alive.
You will be dead soon enough.

WILLIAM SAROYAN

A New Person

Father, thanks to You I get to start
over, fresh and clean, because
You have made me a new person.
I now have a lifetime of new
days to spend any way I choose.
Thank You for Your never-ending
forgiveness. Amen.

Don't Wait

Don't wait until everything is just right. It will never be perfect. There will always be challenges, obstacles and less than perfect conditions. So what. Get started now. With each step you take, you will grow stronger and stronger, more and more skilled, more and more self-confident, and more and more successful.

MARK VICTOR HANSEN

Imagination

The most beautiful world is always
entered through the imagination.
If you wish to be something you
are not—something fine, noble,
good—you shut your eyes, and for
one dreamy moment you are that
which you long to be.

HELEN KELLER

Encourage and Love

Flatter me, and I may not believe
you. Criticize me, and I may not
like you. Ignore me, and I may not
forgive you. Encourage me, and I
will not forget you. Love me and I
may be forced to love you.

WILLIAM ARTHUR WARD

Scripture

When you're looking for some sweetness in a sour life, turn to scripture. The scriptures are God's huge love letter to His own people. As even the newest believer reads attentively, God's mercy becomes clear. Yet a lifelong believer can read the same passage and see something new again and again.

PAMELA MCQUADE

Heaven

Lord, I know there will come a
day when we will be in heaven
with You. I look forward to that
time, and I thank You for the
opportunity to share that time and
place with You. Amen.

An Offering

Take your everyday, ordinary
life—your sleeping, eating, going-
to-work, and walking-around
life—and place it before God as
an offering. Embracing what God
does for you is the best thing you
can do for him.

ROMANS 12:1 MSG

Believe You Can

Men often become what they
believe themselves to be. If I
believe I cannot do something, it
makes me incapable of doing it.
But when I believe I can, then I
acquire the ability to do it even if I
didn't have it in the beginning.

MAHATMA GANDHI

Getting Started

The secret of getting ahead is getting started. The secret of getting started is breaking your complex overwhelming tasks into small manageable tasks, and then starting on the first one.

MARK TWAIN

Love

Love is friendship that has caught
fire. It is quiet understanding,
mutual confidence, sharing and
forgiving. It is loyalty through
good and bad times. It settles for
less than perfection and makes
allowances for human weaknesses.

ANN LANDERS

To God All Praise and Glory!

What God's almighty power
  hath made
His gracious mercy keepeth,
By morning glow or evening shade
His watchful eye ne'er sleepeth.
Within the kingdom of His might,
Lo! All is just and all is right:
To God all praise and glory!

JOHANN J. SCHÜTZ

And Give You Peace

"The LORD bless you and keep you;
the LORD make his face shine upon
you and be gracious to you; the
LORD turn his face toward you and
give you peace."

NUMBERS 6:24–26 NIV

Open Wide

Open wide the windows of our
spirits and fill us full of light;
open wide the door of our hearts
that we may receive and entertain
Thee with all the powers of our
adoration.

CHRISTINA ROSSETTI

A Gentle Word

A gentle word, like summer rain,
may soothe some heart
   and banish pain.
What joy or sadness often springs
from just the simple little things!

WILLA HOEY

Climb Higher

Why should we live halfway up the
hill and swathed in the mists, when
we might have an unclouded sky
with a radiant sun over our heads
if we would climb higher and walk
in the light of His face?

ALEXANDER MACLAREN

No Despair

One of the best safeguards of our
hopes. . .is to be able to mark off
the areas of hopelessness and to
acknowledge them, to face them
directly, not with despair but with
the creative intent of keeping
them from polluting all the areas
of possibility.

WILLIAM F. LYNCH

Those Who Love

Those who love are borne on wings;
they run and are filled with joy;
they are free and unrestricted. . . .
Beyond all things they rest in the
one highest thing, from Whom
streams all that is good.

THOMAS À KEMPIS

I Wish

When you are lonely,
  I wish you love;
When you are down,
  I wish you joy;
When you are troubled,
  I wish you peace;
When things are complicated,
  I wish you simple beauty;
When things are chaotic,
  I wish you inner silence;
At all times I wish you
  the God of hope.

UNKNOWN

By Grace

For it is by grace you have been
saved, through faith—and this
not from yourselves, it is the gift
of God—not by works, so that no
one can boast. For we are God's
workmanship, created in Christ
Jesus to do good works, which God
prepared in advance for us to do.

EPHESIANS 2:8–10 NIV

Wonderful Life

Coming to Jesus brings us new
life. Not just a few more years on
earth or a better way of living,
but real, exciting, wonderful life.
Existence free from the necessity
of constant sin. The ability to do
right things for the right reasons.
Life connected to God Himself.

PAMELA MCQUADE

Obedience

All of God's revealed truths are
sealed until they are opened to
us through obedience. Even the
smallest bit of obedience opens
heaven.

OSWALD CHAMBERS

A Wonderful Name

Jesus. What a wonderful name! It
is the only name we need to call
upon for salvation. I praise You for
being the Way, the Truth, and the
Life, Lord. Amen.

Christian Faith

Christian faith is like a grand
cathedral, with divinely pictured
windows. Standing without, you
can see no glory, nor can imagine
any. But standing within, every
ray of light reveals a harmony of
unspeakable splendors.

NATHANIEL HAWTHORNE

God Knows

God knows everything about us.
And He cares about everything.
Moreover, He can manage every
situation. And He loves us!
Surely this is enough to open the
wellsprings of joy. . . . And joy is
always a source of strength.

HANNAH WHITALL SMITH

By the Grace of God

I am not what I ought to be; I am
not what I wish to be; I am not
what I hope to be, but, by the grace
of God, I am not what I was.

JOHN NEWTON

Our Dwelling Place

When we are told that God, who
is our dwelling place, is also our
fortress, it can only mean one
thing. . .that if we will but live in
our dwelling place, we shall be
perfectly safe and secure.

HANNAH WHITALL SMITH

Laughter

Sense of humor, God's great gift,
causes spirits to uplift;
Helps to make our bodies mend,
lightens burdens, cheers a friend;
Tickles children, elders grin at this
warmth that glows within;
Surely in the great hereafter,
heaven must be full of laughter!

UNKNOWN

All Prepared

Like an open book, you watched
me grow from conception to
birth; all the stages of my life were
spread out before you, the days of
my life all prepared before I'd even
lived one day.

PSALM 139:16 MSG

Welcoming

Lord, You welcomed me into Your
family with love and acceptance.
Help me be as kind to others as
You have been to me—cheerfully
welcoming everyone. Amen.

God Is Great

I belong to the "Great God Party"
and will have nothing to do with
the "Little God Party." Christ does
not want nibblers of the possible,
but grabbers of the impossible.

C. T. STUDD

Unending Praise

May your life become one of glad
and unending praise to the Lord
as you journey through this world,
and in the world that is to come!

TERESA OF AVILA

Come, Thou Fount

Come, Thou Fount of every
  blessing, tune my heart to
  sing Thy grace;
Streams of mercy, never ceasing,
  call for songs of loudest praise.
Teach me some melodious sonnet,
  sung by flaming tongues above;
Praise the mount—I'm fixed upon
  it—mount of Thy redeeming
  love.

ROBERT ROBINSON

His Ability Is Great

If you have a special need today, focus your full attention on the goodness and greatness of your Father rather than on the size of your need. Your need is so small compared to His ability to meet it.

More

More faith in my Savior,
   more sense of His care;
More joy in His service,
   more purpose in prayer. . .
More fit for the kingdom,
   more used would I be;
More blessed and holy,
   more, Savior, like Thee.

PHILIP P. BLISS

Faith and Love

Faith, like light, should always be
simple and unbending; while love,
like warmth, should beam forth
on every side and bend to every
necessity of our brethren.

MARTIN LUTHER

Pressing On

Forgetting what is behind and
straining toward what is ahead, I
press on toward the goal to win the
prize for which God has called me
heavenward in Christ Jesus.

PHILIPPIANS 3:13–14 NIV

He Guides

Father, thank You for Your
promise to guide me in all things
great and small. Your eye is always
on me, keeping me from error and
ensuring that I can always find a
way home to You. Amen.

The Glory of Friendship

The glory of friendship is. . .the
spiritual inspiration that comes
to one when he discovers that
someone else believes in him and
is willing to trust him with his
friendship.

RALPH WALDO EMERSON

Rest, Don't Quit!

When things go wrong,
  as they sometimes will,
When the road you're trudging
  seems all uphill,
When the funds are low
  and the debts are high,
And you want to smile,
  but you have to sigh,
When care is pressing you
  down a bit,
Rest, if you must—
  but don't you quit!

UNKNOWN

Step Out

Let us step into the darkness and
reach out for the hand of God.
The path of faith and darkness
is so much safer than the one we
would choose by sight.

GEORGE MacDONALD

If Only You Ask

Facing a tough time? See it as a chance to learn just how faithful your Lord is. Then thank Him that though you can't rejoice that you face the circumstances, you can be glad He's by your side every step of the way. He will be there for you—if only you ask.

PAMELA McQUADE

Do Not Fear

So do not fear, for I am with you;
do not be dismayed, for I am your
God. I will strengthen you and
help you; I will uphold you with my
righteous right hand.

ISAIAH 41:10 NIV

Today

Today Jesus is working just as
wonderful works as when He
created the heaven and the
earth. His wondrous grace, His
wonderful omnipotence, is for His
child who needs Him and who
trusts Him, even today.

CHARLES E. HURLBURT AND T. C. HORTON

Look It in the Eye

If I were asked to give what I consider the single most useful bit of advice for all humanity it would be this: Expect trouble as an inevitable part of life and when it comes, hold your head high, look it squarely in eye, and say, "I will be bigger than you. You cannot defeat me."

ANN LANDERS

Take Hold

Take hold of this good gift God
has for you. Accept the bad news
that you've sinned, and offer that
wrong up to Him. He'll reply with
the Good News that Jesus died
for it all, and your repentance has
already given you the best His
kingdom has to offer: forgiveness
for every sin.

PAMELA McQUADE

Content through Praise

The thought of You stirs us so
deeply that we cannot be content
unless we praise You, because You
have made us for yourself and our
hearts find no peace until they rest
in You.

St. Augustine

Blessed Assurance

Blessed assurance, Jesus is mine!
Oh, what a foretaste
　of glory divine!
Heir of salvation,
　purchase of God,
Born of His Spirit,
　washed in His blood.

FANNY J. CROSBY

His Great Love

Because of his great love for us,
God, who is rich in mercy, made
us alive with Christ even when we
were dead in transgressions—it is
by grace you have been saved.

EPHESIANS 2:4–5 NIV

Jesus Is Light

I heard the voice of Jesus say:
"I am this dark world's light;
Look unto Me, thy morn shall rise,
and all thy day be bright."
I looked to Jesus, and I found in
Him my Star, my Sun;
And in that light of life, I'll walk
till traveling days are done!

HORATIUS BONAR

Nothing Compares

Nothing can compare to the beauty and greatness of the soul in which our King dwells in His full majesty. No earthly fire can compare with the light of its blazing love. No bastions can compare with its ability to endure forever.

TERESA OF AVILA

Count Your Blessings

Count your blessings;
  name them one by one.
Count your blessings;
  see what God has done!
Count your blessings;
  name them one by one.
Count your many blessings;
  see what God has done!

JOHNSON OATMAN JR.

Friends Help

My friends have made the story of
my life. In a thousand ways they
have turned my limitations into
beautiful privileges and enabled
me to walk serene and happy in the
shadow cast by my deprivation.

HELEN KELLER

Through Every Storm

We shall steer safely through every
storm, so long as our heart is right,
our intention fervent, our courage
steadfast, and our trust fixed on
God.

ST. FRANCIS DE SALES

He Delivers

Lord, I do not know how to deliver
myself from temptation, but You
know the way. You have been there.
When I stumble, I know Your
arms will catch me; if I fall, You
bring me to my feet and guide me
onward. Amen.

Blessing on Blessing

God, who is love—who is, if I
may say it this way, made out of
love—simply cannot help but shed
blessing on blessing upon us. We
do not need to beg, for He simply
cannot help it!

HANNAH WHITALL SMITH

Loving the Lord

My love of You, O Lord, is not
some vague feeling: It is positive
and certain. Your Word struck into
my heart and from that moment I
loved You. Besides this, all about
me, heaven and earth and all
that they contain proclaim that I
should love You.

St. Augustine

Not All

This life is not all. It is an "unfinished symphony". . .with those who know that they are related to God and have felt "the power of an endless life."

HENRY WARD BEECHER

Take Heart

"I have told you these things, so
that in me you may have peace. In
this world you will have trouble.
But take heart! I have overcome
the world."

JOHN 16:33 NIV

Through Hard Times

It's usually through our hard
times, the unexpected and not-
according-to-plan times, that
we experience God in more
intimate ways. We discover an
unquenchable longing to know
Him more.

UNKNOWN

Fear vs. *Faith*

Fear imprisons, faith liberates;
fear paralyzes, faith empowers;
fear disheartens, faith encourages;
fear sickens, faith heals; fear
makes useless, faith makes
serviceable—and most of all, fear
puts hopelessness at the heart of
life, while faith rejoices in its God.

HARRY EMERSON FOSDICK

An Infinite God

An infinite God can give all of
Himself to each of His children.
He does not distribute Himself
that each may have a part, but to
each one He gives all of Himself
as fully as if there were no others.

A. W. TOZER

Working Faith

This is a sane, wholesome, practical working faith: That it is man's business to do the will of God; second, that God Himself takes on the care of that man; and third, that therefore that man ought never to be afraid of anything.

GEORGE MACDONALD

All That We See

God has not made a little universe.
He has made the wide stretches
of space and has put there all the
flaming hosts we see at night, all
the planets, stars, and galaxies.
Wherever we go, let us remind
ourselves that God has made
everything we see. . . . And not
only did God make it all, but He is
present.

FRANCIS A. SCHAEFFER

The God of Love and Peace

May the God of love and peace set your heart at rest and speed you on your journey. May He meanwhile shelter you. . .in the place of complete plenitude where you will repose forever in the vision of peace, in the security of trust, and in the restful enjoyment of His riches.

RAYMOND OF PENYAFORT

A Different Sort of Evidence

Faith does not mean believing
without evidence. It means
believing in realities that go
beyond sense and sight—for which
a totally different sort of evidence
is required.

JOHN BAILLIE

The Inner Fire

In everyone's life, at some time,
our inner fire goes out. It is then
burst into flame by an encounter
with another human being. We
should all be thankful for those
people who rekindle the inner
spirit.

ALBERT SCHWEITZER

His Name Proclaimed

"I have raised you up for this very
purpose, that I might show you my
power and that my name might be
proclaimed in all the earth."

EXODUS 9:16 NIV

Renew Me

As I learn to rest in You, Lord,
renew me. Give me the ability
I need to be patient, no matter
what trouble is around me. Let my
joyful hope and faithful prayers
build up my patience. Amen.

God Seeks You

If you are seeking after God, you may be sure of this: God is seeking you much more. He is the Lover, and you are His beloved. He has promised Himself to you.

JOHN OF THE CROSS

Promises Kept

We may. . .depend upon God's
promises, for. . .he will be as good
as His word. He is so kind that He
cannot deceive us, so true that He
cannot break His promise.

MATTHEW HENRY

So Small a Thing

Is it so small a thing to have
enjoyed the sun, to have lived
light in the spring, to have loved,
to have thought, to have done; to
have advanced true friends?

MATTHEW ARNOLD

Limitless Hope

When we take time to notice the
simple things in life, we never lack
for encouragement. We discover
we are surrounded by limitless
hope that's just wearing everyday
clothes.

ANONYMOUS

His Divine Power

His divine power has given us
everything we need for life and
godliness through our knowledge
of him who called us by his own
glory and goodness.

2 PETER 1:3 NIV

Love Is the Key

Love is the key. Joy is love
singing. Peace is love resting.
Long-suffering is love enduring.
Kindness is love's touch. Goodness
is love's character. Faithfulness is
love's habit. Gentleness is love's
self-forgetfulness. Self-control is
love holding the reins.

DONALD GREY BARNHOUSE

Grace

We know certainly that our God. . .
gives us every grace, every abundant
grace; and though we are so weak
of ourselves, this grace is able to
carry us through every obstacle and
difficulty.

ELIZABETH ANN SETON

A Thankful Spirit

First among the things to be
thankful for is a thankful spirit. . . .
Happy are they who possess this gift!
Blessings may fail and fortunes vary,
but the thankful heart remains.

UNKNOWN

As Flowers

As flowers carry dewdrops,
trembling on the edges of the
petals and ready to fall at the
first waft of the wind or brush of
bird, so the heart should carry its
beaded words of thanksgiving. At
the first breath of heavenly flavor,
let down the shower, perfumed
with the heart's gratitude.

HENRY WARD BEECHER

Thanksgiving

Enter his gates with thanksgiving
and his courts with praise; give
thanks to him and praise his name.
For the LORD is good and his love
endures forever; his faithfulness
continues through all generations.

PSALM 100:4–5 NIV

A Loving Thought

If instead of a gem, or even a
flower, we should cast the gift of a
loving thought into the heart of a
friend, that would be giving as the
angels give.

GEORGE MACDONALD

He Answers

Do you long for help from God?
Your desire is in the right place.
Just ask, then trust He will answer.
Tomorrow may not solve every
problem, but you can know that
help is on the way. You've put your
faith in the eternal God who never
fails. Talk to Him this morning,
and watch help appear.

PAMELA MCQUADE

Hope Thou

Knowest thou not that day follows
night, that flood comes after ebb,
that spring and summer succeed
winter? Hope thou then! Hope
thou ever! God fails thee not.

CHARLES H. SPURGEON

May the Sun Always Shine

May the sun always shine on your
windowpane; may a rainbow be
certain to follow each rain; may
the hand of a friend always be near
you; may God fill your heart with
gladness to cheer you.

IRISH BLESSING

Immeasurable Love

We are so preciously loved by God
that we cannot comprehend it.
No created being can ever know
how much and how sweetly and
tenderly God loves them. It is only
with the help of His grace that we
are able to persevere in spiritual
contemplation with endless
wonder at His high, surpassing,
immeasurable love which our Lord
in His goodness has for us.

JULIAN OF NORWICH

Not Alone

Lord, direct me daily to accept
and apply the strength that You've
offered, so that I will truly have
the gentle spirit that You intend
me to have. Thank You, Jesus, that
I don't have to do this on my own.
Amen.

How Can I Keep from Singing?

My life flows on in endless song;
Above earth's lamentation
I hear the sweet though
   far-off hymn
That hails a new creation. . . .
Since God is Lord of
   heaven and earth,
How can I keep from singing?

UNKNOWN

Promise of a Better Day

From far beyond our world of
trouble and care and change, our
Lord shines with undimmed light,
a radiant, guiding Start to all who
will follow Him—a morning Star,
promise of a better day.

CHARLES E. HURLBURT AND T. C. HORTON

Surprises

In all our lives, in many simple,
familiar, homely ways, God
infuses this element of joy
from the surprises of life, which
unexpectedly brighten our days,
and fill our eyes with light.

HENRY WADSWORTH LONGFELLOW

Wonderful Things

God has wonderful things in mind
for you. If you ask, He'll show you
what gifts He's given you and how
He wants you to bless others with
them. Don't wait until eternity to
experience the joys and delights
of faith—share some of that good
news today!

PAMELA MCQUADE

The Son of the Most High

"You will be with child and give birth to a son, and you are to give him the name Jesus. He will be great and will be called the Son of the Most High. The Lord God will give him the throne of his father David, and. . .his kingdom will never end."

LUKE 1:31–33 NIV

Just Be

Don't get so busy that you forget
to simply *be*. Sometimes the best
way to stop being overwhelmed by
life is to simply step back, take a
day. . .or an hour. . .or a moment,
and notice all that God is doing in
your life.

ELLYN SANNA

Jesus

The word which became flesh has
a name. And approaching this day
of days, at this season of seasons,
let the splendor of that Man above
men sparkle upon your lips. Jesus.

JAMES SMETHAM

From Faith to Faith

Trust in your Redeemer's strength. . .
exercise what faith you have, and by
and by He shall rise upon you with
healing beneath His wings. Go from
faith to faith and you shall receive
blessing upon blessing.

CHARLES H. SPURGEON

Without Fear

We walk without fear, full of hope
and courage and strength to do
His will, waiting for the endless
good which He is always giving as
fast as He can get us able to take
it in.

GEORGE MACDONALD

His Touch

The Lord's chief desire is to reveal
Himself to you and, in order for
Him to do that, He gives you
abundant grace. The Lord gives
you the experience of enjoying His
presence. He touches you, and His
touch is so delightful that, more
than ever, you are drawn inwardly
to Him.

MADAME JEANNE GUYON

He Will Provide

Each of us may be sure that if
God sends us on stony paths He
will provide us with strong shoes,
and He will not send us out on
any journey for which He does not
equip us well.

ALEXANDER MACLAREN

A Savior Born

"Do not be afraid. I bring you good
news of great joy that will be for
all the people. Today in the town
of David a Savior has been born to
you; he is Christ the Lord."

LUKE 2:10–11 NIV

God Came to Us

God came to us because God
wanted to join us on the road, to
listen to our story, and to help us
realize that we are not walking
in circles but moving toward the
house of peace and joy.

THOMAS MERTON

In His Hands

Heavenly Father, I long for Your
peace in my heart. Please take
every anxious thread, every tightly
pulled knot of uncertainty, sorrow,
conflict, and disappointment into
Your gentle, loving hands. Amen.

A Garden

To know someone here or there
with whom you feel there is an
understanding in spite of distances
or thoughts unexpressed—that
can make of this earth a garden.

JOHANN WOLFGANG VON GOETHE

Eternity

Eternity is the divine treasure
house, and hope is the window,
by means of which mortals are
permitted to see, as through a glass
darkly, the things which God is
preparing.

WILLIAM MOUNTFORD

Happiness

Happiness is a sunbeam. . . . When
it strikes a kindred heart, like the
converged lights upon a mirror,
it reflects itself with redoubled
brightness. It is not perfected until
it is shared.

JANE PORTER

That It Should Take Place in Me

We are celebrating the feast of the Eternal Birth which God the Father has borne and never ceases to bear in all eternity. . . . But if it takes not place in me, what avails it? Everything lies in this, that it should take place in me.

MEISTER ECKHART

Humble Yourself

"If my people, who are called by my name, will humble themselves and pray and seek my face and turn from their wicked ways, then will I hear from heaven and will forgive their sin and will heal their land."

2 CHRONICLES 7:14 NIV

His Mystery, Your Promise

Trust God where you cannot trace Him. Do not try to penetrate the clouds He brings over you; rather look to the bow that is on it. The mystery is God's; the promise is yours.

JOHN R. MACDUFF

Born to Deliver

Born Thy people to deliver,
Born a child and yet a king.
Born to reign in us forever,
Now Thy gracious kingdom bring.
By Thine own eternal Spirit
Rule in all our hearts alone;
By Thine all sufficient merit,
Raise us to Thy glorious throne.

CHARLES WESLEY

When Christ Was Born

A thrill of hope
   the weary world rejoices,
For yonder breaks
   a new and glorious morn.
Fall on your knees,
   O, hear the angel voices.
O night divine, O night
   when Christ was born!

JOHN S. DWIGHT

Prince of Wholeness

For a child has been born—for
us! the gift of a son—for us!
He'll take over the running of the
world. His names will be: Amazing
Counselor, Strong God, Eternal
Father, Prince of Wholeness.
His ruling authority will grow,
and there'll be no limits to the
wholeness he brings.

ISAIAH 9:6–7 MSG

Heaven for Us All

Many merry Christmases, many
happy New Years. Unbroken
friendships, great accumulations
of cheerful recollections and
affections on earth, and heaven
for us all.

CHARLES DICKENS

The Spirit of Love

You will find as you look back
upon your life that the moments
when you have truly lived are the
moments when you have done
things in the spirit of love.

HENRY DRUMMOND

Creator of Light

O God, creator of light: at the rising of Your sun this morning, let the greatest of all lights, Your love, rise like the sun within our hearts.

ARMENIAN APOSTOLIC CHURCH

What God Will Do

You never can measure what God
will do through you. . . . Keep your
relationship right with Him, then
whatever circumstances you are in,
and whoever you meet day by day,
He is pouring rivers of living water
through you.

OSWALD CHAMBERS

In God's Heart

A room of quiet—
  a temple of peace;
A home of faith—
  where doubtings cease;
A house of comfort—
  where hope is given;
A source of strength—
  to make earth heaven;
A shrine of worship—
  a place to pray—
I found all this—
  in God's heart today.

UNKNOWN

Never-ending Blessings

Heavenly Father, I have so much
to be thankful for. My list of
blessings is never-ending. May
I never fail to praise You and to
thank You for the many blessings
You have given to me. Amen.

Scripture Index

OLD TESTAMENT

NEW TESTAMENT